HAL•LEONARD
INSTRUMENTAL PLAY-ALONG

ALTO SAX

CHART HITS OF '06-'07

D1447476

HOW TO USE THE CD ACCOMPANIMENT:
A MELODY CUE APPEARS ON THE RIGHT CHANNEL ONLY. IF YOUR
CD PLAYER HAS A BALANCE ADJUSTMENT, YOU CAN ADJUST THE
VOLUME OF THE MELODY BY TURNING DOWN THE RIGHT CHANNEL.

ISBN-13: 978-1-4234-2653-0
ISBN-10: 1-4234-2653-3

HAL•LEONARD®
CORPORATION

7777 W. BLUEMOUND RD. P.O. BOX 13819 MILWAUKEE, WI 53213

Visit Hal Leonard Online at
www.halleonard.com

BAD DAY

ALTO SAX

Words and Music by
DANIEL POWTER

❷ BLACK HORSE
AND THE CHERRY TREE

ALTO SAX

Words and Music by
KATIE TUNSTALL

❸ CALL ME WHEN YOU'RE SOBER

ALTO SAX

Words and Music by TERRY BALSAMO
and AMY LEE

◆ CRAZY

Words and Music by BRIAN BURTON,
THOMAS CALLAWAY, GIANPIERO REVERBERI
and GIANFRANCO REVERBERI

ALTO SAX

❖5 HOW TO SAVE A LIFE

ALTO SAX

Words and Music by JOSEPH KING
and ISAAC SLADE

◆ JESUS TAKE THE WHEEL

ALTO SAX

Words and Music by BRETT JAMES,
GORDIE SAMPSON and HILLARY LINDSEY

⑦ KEEP HOLDING ON

from the Twentieth Century Fox Motion Picture ERAGON

ALTO SAX

Words and Music by AVRIL LAVIGNE
and LUKAS GOTTWALD

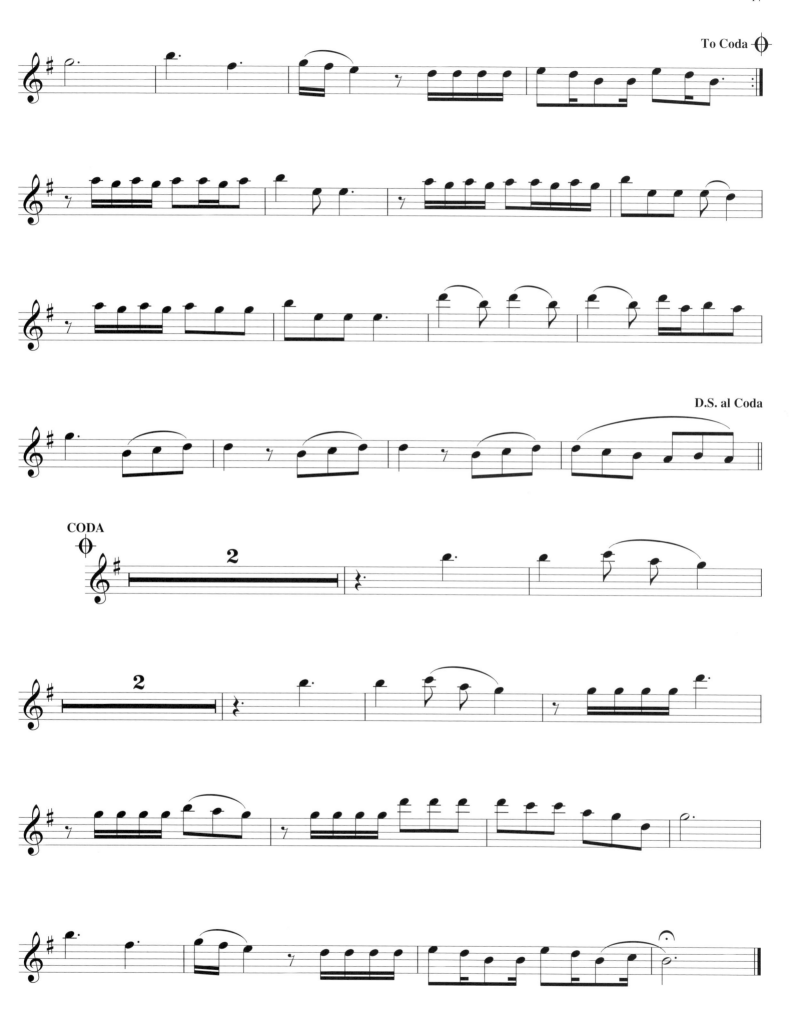

8 LIPS OF AN ANGEL

ALTO SAX

Words and Music by AUSTIN WINKLER,
ROSS HANSON, LLOYD GARVEY, MARK KING,
MICHAEL RODDEN and BRIAN HOWES

◆ WHAT HURTS THE MOST

ALTO SAX

Words and Music by STEVE ROBSON
and JEFFREY STEELE

◆⑨ LISTEN

from the Motion Picture DREAMGIRLS

ALTO SAX

Words and Music by HENRY KRIEGER, ANNE PREVEN,
SCOTT CUTLER and BEYONCÉ KNOWLES

MOVE ALONG

ALTO SAX

Words and Music by TYSON RITTER
and NICK WHEELER

mp-f

2

Play 4 times

NOTHING LEFT TO LOSE

ALTO SAX

Words and Music by
MATHEW KEARNEY

⑫ UNFAITHFUL

ALTO SAX

Words and Music by MIKKEL ERIKSEN,
TOR ERIK HERMANSEN and SHAFFER SMITH

🔷13 UNWRITTEN

ALTO SAX

Words and Music by NATASHA BEDINGFIELD,
DANIELLE BRISEBOIS and WAYNE RODRIGUES

Medium Pop

15 YOU'RE BEAUTIFUL

ALTO SAX

Words and Music by JAMES BLUNT,
SACHA SCARBECK and AMANDA GHOST